The A–Z of Lying

The A to Z of Lying

Rash Ryder

MAINSTREAM
PUBLISHING

EDINBURGH AND LONDON

First published in Great Britain in 1997 by
MAINSTREAM PUBLISHING COMPANY (EDINBURGH) LTD
7 Albany Street
Edinburgh EH1 3UG

First published in Australia in 1996 by Pan Macmillan Australia Pty Limited

ISBN 1 85158 985 6

A catalogue record for this book is available from the British Library

Designed by Jenny Haig
Typeset in Garamond and Gill Sans
Printed and bound in Finland by WSOY

Monday 18th October, 1999

Dedicated to my good looks
and sheer charm

Jason,

I hope you have a great 30th birthday. I wish you all the best and hope you race driving career takes off.....

lots of love,

Thomm

Very special thanks to Trevor Crook, Vince Sorrenti
and all at my publishers

Rash Ryder first tore into the list of the world's richest people in 1994 at the number one position with an estimated net worth of £4.7 billion. He attributes his wealth and success to a straightforward dialogue with people – many examples of which appear in this book.

Those who have read his work testify that they have increased their wealth, have improved personal relationships and phenomenally increased the size of their sex organs.

Many people have reaped the benefits of Rash's insights, including Members of Parliament, lawyers, advocates and television personalities.

The Ten Commandments

1. Keep a straight face

2. Look them straight in the eye

3. Always believe in what you've said

4. Always remember what you've said

5. Always remember who you've said it to

6. Never think of the consequences

7. When stumped, consult this book

8. Never lie while actually consulting this book

9. Never come clean

10. After getting away with the lie, make sure you take time to savour the experience

Topless bathers

ACCIDENTS

It's of paramount importance, whether talking to the police, the insurance company, the judge or the victim to have a back-up of top quality 'pork pies'.

Whenever there is an accident, always tell a lie, unless the accident falls in your favour.

Car accidents
It's important to remember when involved in a car accident not to move, as it is obvious that *you* have whiplash as well as your other three passengers.

In case of a head on, red light, or out of control:

A BEE STUNG ME.
(Smear a bit of honey on your head or, if you have small tits, point to your nipples and say, 'Look, it stung me twice.')

I SWERVED BECAUSE A DOG RAN ON THE ROAD.
(Yeah, I was trying to hit it.)

THERE WAS A LOT OF OIL ON THE ROAD.
(Can use this on a pedestrian crossing.)

SORRY, MATE, I DIDN'T SEE YOU.
(Say this while looking slightly away from the person and
stepping out of the car with dark sunglasses, a hat and a
cane. Works well if you drive a Volvo.)

I DROPPED A CIGARETTE ON MY CROTCH.
(Stub a cigarette out on your crotch before the police get
there.)

A CHICKEN WAS CROSSING THE ROAD AND I COULDN'T
STOP LAUGHING.
(What traffic cop – the one jammed under your back
wheels?)

SORRY, MATE, THE SUN WAS IN MY EYES.
(Never use this one at night.)

SORRY, MATE, MY WINDSCREEN WIPERS AREN'T WORKING.
(Never use this if you're riding a motor bike or if you are a
pedestrian.)

SORRY, MY GIRLFRIEND WAS GIVING ME HEAD . . . I MEAN MY
HEAD A RUB BECAUSE I BUMPED IT.

Red Lights

OFFICER, WAS IT GREEN?

IT WAS GREEN.

I'M TELLING YOU IT WAS GREEN.

THERE COULD HAVE BEEN A TINGE OF ORANGE IN IT.

OKAY, IT WAS ORANGE, BUT NO WAY WAS IT RED.

LISTEN, IT TURNED RED WHEN I WAS HALFWAY THROUGH IT.

WOULD YOU BELIEVE – I'M COLOUR BLIND?

If colour blind:

OFFICER, IT WAS BLACK.

IT WAS BLACK.

I'M TELLING YOU, IT WAS BLACK.

Work accidents

When accidents happen at work, always blame it on someone junior to yourself.

I TOLD THAT IDIOT WHAT TO DO.

I TOLD THAT IDIOT WHAT *NOT* TO DO.

WHO WAS THE IDIOT THAT DID THIS?

WHERE'S THAT IDIOT APPRENTICE?

THESE TOOLS ARE HOPELESS.
(To add weight to your argument, give the tools a minute's notice.)

Hiding the fact:

MATE, I DON'T KNOW WHAT YOU'RE TALKING ABOUT.
(Neither do I.)

If you work alone, blame it on the alignment of the planets. If you drop something, blame Isaac Newton for inventing gravity.

Household accidents
Any household accident can be blamed on the pet, because they've got no defence.
Anything that's broken:

THE DOG MUST HAVE DONE IT WITH ITS TAIL.
(Make sure your dog hasn't had its tail docked.)

I'VE GOT A SNEAKING SUSPICION IT WAS THE GOLDFISH.
(Make sure you place a hammer and chainsaw in the goldfish bowl.)

IT MUST HAVE BEEN THE WIND.

IT WAS THE BULL FROM THE CHINA SHOP.
(Buy a heap of steaks from the butcher's shop and throw them around your house and tell them how you killed the bull by hacking it to death.)

THE CAT DID IT.

WE'VE BEEN BURGLED.
(Don't say this wearing a balaclava.)

Cooking accidents

THE KITCHEN WAS ON FIRE BEFORE I STARTED.
(Be optimistic – if you've ever tasted my cooking, the fire was a godsend.)

WOULD YOU BELIEVE THE KITCHEN WAS ON FIRE WHEN I BOUGHT THE HOUSE?
(Don't tell them you were an owner/builder.)

I WAS JUST TESTING THE SMOKE DETECTORS.

IT'S MEANT TO BE BLACK.

I DIDN'T REALISE I HAD TO KILL THE CHICKEN BEFORE I MICROWAVED IT.

ADULTERY

Since the beginning of time, men and women have committed adultery. Practically every lie under the sun has been used. Subsequently, A-Grade lying is now required. Refer to the Ten Commandments.

If caught in the act, say this with total conviction:

IT'S PURELY PLATONIC.

If this fails, resort to the following:

IT'S PURELY SEXUAL.

I THOUGHT IT WAS YOU.
(Because they were pitiful also.)

PLEAD IGNORANCE – WHAT WOMAN, WHAT SUITCASE,

WHAT TICKETS TO RIO?

I ONLY DID IT TO REMIND ME OF HOW MUCH I LOVE YOU
AND HOW GOOD YOU REALLY ARE IN BED.
(Don't say this in front of the person you just had sex
with.)

IT'S YOUR FAULT, BECAUSE YOU NEVER SHOW ME ANY
AFFECTION.
(Not a good line if you get busted having bondage and
discipline.)

I'LL NEVER DO IT AGAIN.
(Get caught, that is.)

IT'S YOUR FAULT.
(Put it back on them, it's your last resort.)

AGENTS

DON'T CALL US – WE'LL CALL YOU.

THE CHEQUE'S IN THE MAIL.
(Shit, yeah.)

THEY'RE IN A MEETING AT THE MOMENT, SO THEY WILL CALL YOU AFTER THEY FINISH.
(1999)

I'M SORRY, WE DON'T RECEIVE BUSINESS CALLS DURING WORKING HOURS.
(If you hear someone in the background say, 'Not this idiot again', it's time for a career change.)

DID YOU THINK WE WERE GETTING 12.5 PER CENT?

WE REPRESENT ELVIS, HENDRIX, BUDDY HOLLY, JANIS, KURT COBAIN AND MELISSA TKAUTZ.

If your agent answers the phone with 'Hello, Abdulla's Charcoal Chicken Shop', there's a good chance he doesn't want to talk to you.

A L C O H O L

With alcohol, one drink is too many and 100 is not enough. Alcohol will make you blatantly lie and boast – especially when confronting the opposite sex.

Some of the more common lies you should not use but will:

I'VE ONLY HAD ONE.

I'VE ONLY HAD TWO.

I'VE HAD A FEW – NOT THAT MANY.

SOMEONE MUST HAVE PUT SOMETHING IN MY DRINK.

IS THAT SOMEONE *IN* MY DRINK?

I'M NOT PISSED.
(I always act like a total idiot.)

I COULD DRINK TEN OF THEM EASY.
(Don't make a bet unless it's water.)

SOMEONE ELSE THREW UP ON THE FRONT OF MY SHIRT.
(Make sure there's not a piece of carrot hanging out of
your nose.)

I LOVE YOU.
(You know you're really pissed when you say this.)

I THINK YOU'RE BEAUTIFUL.
(Try not to slur.)

I OWN A PORSCHE.

WOULD YOU LIKE TO STAR IN MY MOVIE?

OF COURSE I'LL RESPECT YOU IN THE MORNING.
(Because I won't be here.)

If they ask you if you remember their name:

OF COURSE I REMEMBER YOUR NAME.
(Who are you?)

DON'T INSULT ME.

WE JUST SHARED AN UNBELIEVABLE SEXUAL EXPERIENCE,

SOMETHING THAT I'LL ALWAYS TREASURE AND YOU ASK ME IF I REMEMBER YOUR NAME?

IT'S WRITTEN ON EVERY TOILET WALL IN THE CITY. HOW COULD I FORGET IT?

FORGET YOUR NAME! HOW COULD I FORGET YOUR NAME? I'VE ALREADY GIVEN IT TO TEN OF MY FRIENDS.

If caught with your head down a toilet bowl:

I'M NOT PISSED, I'VE JUST COME HERE TO THINK.

Appointments

SORRY, I GOT MY DAYS MIXED UP.
(And weeks and years.)

THE TRAFFIC WAS HORRIFIC.
(Make sure you don't live next door.)

YOU TOLD ME THREE O'CLOCK NOT TWO O'CLOCK.
(Make sure your appointment isn't for one o'clock.)

WOULD YOU BELIEVE MY CAR BROKE DOWN, I WAS THEN
KIDNAPPED BY ALIENS IN A UFO AND WHEN I RETURNED
TO EARTH THREE HOURS HAD ELAPSED?

SORRY, I CAN'T MAKE IT TODAY AS I'M FEELING ILL.
(This doesn't work on doctors' appointments.)

SORRY, THE TRAIN GOT A FLAT.

SORRY, OUR BUS WAS HIJACKED.

SORRY I'M LATE.
(I don't consider this appointment remotely important.)

SORRY, I COULDN'T FIND THE BUILDING.
(Believable if your appointment is with an optometrist.)

If asked by a nurse, 'Have you made an appointment?':

YEAH, THREE DAYS AGO, I RANG UP AND BOOKED
BECAUSE I THOUGHT ON FRIDAY NIGHT I MIGHT JUST STAB
MYSELF EIGHT TIMES AT THE LOCAL PUB, THEN DRIVE TO
THE HOSPITAL DYING FROM LACK OF BLOOD.

Sore leg

B ALDING P EOPLE

I'D TAKE THAT WIG BACK IF I WAS YOU – IT'S GOT A HOLE IN IT.

LOOK – HE'S BEEN BRUSHING HIS HAIR FOR THREE HOURS AND HE'S FORGOTTEN TO BRING IT.

I DIDN'T EVEN REALISE YOU WERE WEARING A WIG.
(From a distance, say 200 metres.)

B A N K S

Getting a loan

Make sure the dole form in your top pocket is well concealed. Try not to ask the bank manager for a £5 advance as you are leaving. If all else fails, offer some vigorous oral sex.

I HAVE TWO JOBS.

I DON'T REALLY NEED THE LOAN. IT'S JUST THAT ALL MY MONEY IS TIED UP IN OFFSHORE DRILLING AT THE MOMENT.

Note: Brag about your Porsche, your 20-bedroom house and your yacht.

Note: If they ask you what sort of security you have, don't say Social.

YOU'LL HAVE YOUR MONEY BACK IN NO TIME AT ALL.
(*At all* is about right.)

Kiss your bank manager when you meet him. Refer to
him as 'Your Holiness' at every opportunity.

Giving a loan
If you're the manager:

I'M SORRY, I'M ON WORK EXPERIENCE.

OUR BANK JUST RAN OUT OF MONEY.
(As soon as you walked in.)

I WAS HOPING *YOU* COULD GIVE *US* A LOAN.

SORRY, I'M THE CLEANER.

WHAT DO YOU THINK THIS IS – A CHARITY?

YOU HAVE A VERY ATTRACTIVE WIFE! I'M SURE WE CAN
WORK SOMETHING OUT.

THIS IS THE DEAL. WE'LL LEND YOU ENOUGH MONEY SO
THAT YOU CAN'T POSSIBLY PAY IT BACK. IF YOU DO PAY IT
BACK, THE PROPERTY WILL HAVE COST YOU FOUR TIMES
WHAT IT'S WORTH. CHANCES ARE, YOU'LL FALL BEHIND IN
PAYMENTS. WE'LL GET THE HOUSE AND YOUR WIFE WILL
RUN OFF WITH AN INSURANCE SALESMAN. MANICALLY
DEPRESSED, YOU'LL HIT THE BOTTLE, BEFORE FINALLY

ENDING IT ALL . . . THAT'S OKAY, THERE'S NO NEED TO THANK ME.

B

B L I N D   D A T E

If wishing to abandon ship:

EXCUSE ME – I'VE JUST GOT TO GO AND MAKE AN
OVERSEAS PHONE CALL.
(Don't tell them you're actually going overseas to make it.)

I REALLY LIKE YOU, BUT THE ONLY REASON I CAME ON
THIS DATE WAS BECAUSE I THOUGHT YOU WERE
ACTUALLY BLIND.
(I'm starting to wish I was now.)

I JUST REMEMBERED – I THINK I LEFT THE IRON ON AT
HOME.
(Two minutes prior to stating this, ring the fire brigade
and tell them there's a fire about two blocks away from
the restaurant you're dining at so when the fire brigade

rushes past three minutes later, it's a lot more convincing.)

Tell them the relationship has no future because you have terminal cancer. If they ask, 'How terminal?', reply, 'Any minute now!'

Tell them to stand in a corner somewhere and ask them what they'll be wearing. Drive past, and if they're hideous just keep going.

B

BODY ODOUR

WHAT STINKS? IT MUST BE YOU, YOU FILTHY BASTARD.
(Put it straight to them.)

WHAT STINKS? IT MUST BE THIS BOOK WE'RE READING.

I CAN'T SMELL A THING.
(Don't say this while picking your nose.)

THE REASON I STINK IS BECAUSE I HAVE AN ALLERGY TO
SOAP AND A FEAR OF WATER, AND I DON'T USE A
DEODORANT BECAUSE OF THE OZONE LAYER.

THIS IS THE LAST TIME I LIVE NEXT TO THE ABATTOIRS.
Note: Try and pretend that the smell of a sweat-encrusted
jockstrap is really quite pleasant.

Booze Bust

I CAN'T BLOW INTO THE BAG BECAUSE I'M AN ASTHMATIC.

I CAN'T GIVE YOU A BLOOD SAMPLE BECAUSE I'M A
HAEMOPHILIAC.

I CAN'T WALK THE WHITE LINE BECAUSE I'M TOO PISSED.
(Note: Use this as your last resort.)

I JUST PULLED OVER TO BUY SOME ALCOHOL.
(Use this when you're straight and act drunk – when you
keep giving a reading of 0.00 they will get really pissed off.)

DRUNK? RUBBISH. I OFTEN SWERVE TO AVOID ONCOMING
TRAFFIC, GO ACROSS THE MEDIAN STRIP, CLEAN UP A
COUPLE OF PEDESTRIANS, ROLL THE CAR AND HAVE IT
BURST INTO FLAMES.

Get a passenger in the car to have a fake epileptic fit. Tell the officer you're in a hurry to get them to hospital. Even ask for a police escort because at least you can't get pulled over by any other police.

BREAKING-UP LIES

CAN WE JUST BE FRIENDS?

THERE'S NO ONE ELSE, I JUST WANT TO BE ALONE.

Corn on the cobb

C H A R I T I E S

SORRY – I HAVEN'T GOT ANY SPARE CHANGE.

SORRY – I'M ON THE DOLE.
(Make sure you use this some time after midday.)

I'D LIKE TO GIVE YOU SOME MONEY, BUT I HAVEN'T EATEN IN THREE DAYS MYSELF.
(Make sure you're not talking with a mouthful.)

CHARITY BEGINS AT HOME, AND YOU'RE NOW IN MY HOME SO COUGH UP.

OH – I GAVE AT THE OFFICE.

If confronted in the office:

OH – I GAVE IN THE STREET.

Pretend you're deaf and dumb and can't understand them which, let's face it, will probably be pretty easy.

C

C O U R T

I'M INNOCENT.

I'M INNOCENT.
(When in doubt just keep using this one.)

THAT'S HIM THERE.
(Don't point to the judge.)

I DON'T KNOW WHAT YOU'RE TALKING ABOUT.
(Don't say this when they're asking your name.)

I DON'T KNOW WHAT YOU'RE TALKING ABOUT.
(Can you mime?)

HE MADE ME DO IT.

(Don't say this if the victim is bound, gagged and blindfolded.)

I'VE NEVER SEEN THAT PERSON BEFORE IN MY LIFE.
(Make sure they're not holding up a mirror.)

I'M GUILTY.
(If guilty is the lie you use, you're an idiot.)

I'VE BEEN FRAMED.
(Give your testimony hanging from the wall. If you notice the jury playing backgammon during it, you're in big trouble.)

I DON'T REMEMBER.
(Where am I, anyway?)

To get off jury service
I KNOW THE ACCUSED.

I AM THE ACCUSED.

I DID IT.

Taking the oath
I SWEAR TO TELL THE TRUTH, THE WHOLE TRUTH AND NOTHING BUT THE TRUTH, SO HELP ME, GOD.
(Don't tell them you're an atheist.)

Dog pound

DATING

HI, I'D LIKE TO TAKE YOU OUT ONE DAY ON MY LUXURY YACHT.

LET'S GO FOR A TRIP IN MY LEARJET.
(Buy two tickets on a mystery flight and take them on it.)

SORRY, I CAN'T MAKE IT TONIGHT – MY HUSBAND/WIFE HAS COME HOME.

SORRY, I'M GAY.

I'M CELIBATE.
(Guaranteed to piss them off.)

SORRY, I CAN'T MAKE IT TONIGHT – MUM'S COOKING A LAMB ROAST.

SORRY, I TOTALLY FORGOT ABOUT IT.
(And you – who is this?)

D

D E A T H

Explaining to the kids

DADDY'S GONE TO SLEEP.

(An intelligent child may reply: 'Oh, really? I thought he suffered a cardiac infarction with a total respiratory collapse.')

Try explaining indirectly:

LISTEN, KID, DO YOU KNOW ABOUT YOUR FATHER'S LIFE INSURANCE POLICY? WELL, WE COLLECT IN THREE WEEKS.

HEY, KID, YOU KNOW YOUR DAD'S FAVOURITE CHAIR? WELL, FEEL FREE TO USE IT.

HEY, JOHNNY, CAN YOU GO TO THE SHOP FOR SOME MILK?

OH YEAH, ON YOUR WAY BACK COULD YOU BUY A
WREATH?

HEY KIDS, DO YOU REMEMBER HOW MUCH YOU SAID YOU
WANTED TO KNOW YOUR 'INNER FATHER'? – GREAT,
BECAUSE WE'VE BEEN INVITED TO THE AUTOPSY.

D

D I E T I N G

I HAVE LARGE BONES.
(Yeah, sure, have you ever seen a fat skeleton?)

I HAVE A GLANDULAR PROBLEM.
(Stop kidding yourself.)

I'M STARTING A DIET FIRST THING IN THE MORNING.
(Most people say this so they can stuff themselves the
night before.)

ONE MORE WON'T HURT.
(As long as you're not talking about a whole cow.)

ALL THOSE CHOCOLATE CAKES IN THE FRIDGE ARE IN
CASE A FRIEND DROPS OVER.

(No one's that popular.)

I HARDLY EAT A THING.
(Things must be really big then.)

THESE AREN'T FATTENING.
(When you eat six boxes of them they are, though.)

I HEARD SEX IS REALLY GOOD FOR LOSING WEIGHT.
(You must be a virgin then.)

When you go off your diet, remember that meals aren't retrospective.

I THREW UP BECAUSE I WAS SICK.

GIVE ME THREE CHICKENS, CHIPS, TWO SLICES OF CHOCOLATE CAKE WITH ICE-CREAM, PLUS WHATEVER THAT PERSON OVER THERE IS EATING AND A COKE. OH, MAKE THAT A *DIET* COKE, AS I'M WATCHING MY WEIGHT.

D

D O C T O R

NO, I DON'T NEED STITCHES.
(Not a wise move if your arm or leg is hanging off.)

I CAN'T HAVE A NEEDLE BECAUSE:
* I'M ALLERGIC TO STEEL.
* I'M ALLERGIC TO PAIN.
* I'M ALLERGIC TO BEING ALLERGIC.

I FEEL FINE, DOC.
(Don't say this if you're partially decapitated.)

DOC – COULD I HAVE ANOTHER SHOT OF MORPHINE
BECAUSE I'M IN A LOT OF PAIN?
(Try not to giggle while saying this.)

I'M ALLERGIC TO RUBBER GLOVES.
(So's my bum.)

I NEED SOMETHING TO HELP ME SLEEP.
(Because the uppers I scored off you are too strong.)

DOC – I REALLY NEED AN ANAESTHETIC.
(Save this for when you receive the bill.)

D

DRUGS

When buying drugs:

MATE, I'LL BRING YOU THE MONEY FIRST THING IN THE MORNING.
(*Never* believe this. If they do, go for it.)

Marijuana
Never try and lie while affected by dope. You will be so paranoid that even if you get away with the lie, you probably won't sleep for the next two days.

When mum finds the bong
OH, THAT'S MY SCIENCE EXPERIMENT.

Ecstasy
It will be quite obvious to you by now that you love

everyone and there is no way in the world you could lie to them.

Speed
IT DIDN'T WORK.

Heroin
People on heroin are the best liars on earth. Do listen to everything they've got to say. Check for your wallet before leaving.

Cocaine
People on cocaine are compulsive liars and the most boring people to talk to. They will consistently talk about themselves and how good they are. This is commonly known as 'I' disease.

LSD
EXCUSE ME, DID YOU JUST SEE THAT THREE-HEADED COW FLY PAST?

I'M NOT AN ADDICT.

MATE, I HAVEN'T HAD ANY OF THAT SHIT FOR MONTHS.
(Yeah, that's why you've just fallen asleep . . . hello.)

Chucking a brown eye

E X E R C I S E

JOGGING IS BAD FOR YOU.
(Get the rest of the family to jog instead. It will make them that much quicker when they run for the ambulance.)

I ALWAYS EXERCISE AS I QUITE ENJOY UNBEARABLE CHEST PAIN, INABILITY TO BREATHE AND MY HEAD SLAMMING INTO A CEMENT FLOOR. I DON'T EVEN MIND TURNING BLUE, AS IT BLENDS WELL WITH THE WALLPAPER.

I CAN'T EXERCISE TODAY AS I'M FLAT OUT.
(On my back.)

I'LL START TOMORROW.

I'M FEELING A BIT ILL TODAY.

51

(Because I've eaten too much.)

I DID 12 SIT-UPS THIS MORNING.
(Trying to get out of bed.)

SEX IS EQUIVALENT TO A TEN-KILOMETRE RUN.
(In your case it's equivalent to ten kilometres by public transport.)

Fishin' chips

FARTING

IT WASN'T ME.
(About the most common excuse, but who can prove it?)

WHERE'S THAT DOG?
(I think it's up your arse.)

OH POO – WHO DID THAT?
(Another classic. Nine times out of ten the person blaming the others is the culprit.)

IT'S THAT NEW UNLEADED PETROL I'M USING.
(Don't use this if the engine isn't running.)

I CAN SMELL SHIT – SOMEONE MUST HAVE STOOD IN DOG POO.

(That will keep them guessing long enough for the fart to disperse.)

Blame any *old* person in the room, because:
* Everyone knows they smell.
* They won't hear you blaming them.
* Who cares if they do anyway?

I DID NOT FART – I HAVE SHIT MYSELF SOMEWHAT, THOUGH.

Women farting:
WE NEVER BREAK WIND.
(Oh no, and we also hate going shopping.)

F

FIGHTING

I COULD HAVE DONE HIM.
(If it hadn't been for those six lucky punches.)

IF YOU THINK *I* LOOK BAD YOU SHOULD TAKE A LOOK AT
THE OTHER BLOKE.
(We did and that hair out of place must be causing him
agony.)

I WALKED INTO A DOOR.
(Yeah, I can see the door dancing with your girlfriend.)

WHAT ARE *YOU* LOOKING AT, MATE?
(Don't say this if they look like Marty Feldman. If he
looks remarkably like an ambulanceman the fight is
already over.)

I WON.
(Not to be used in Intensive Care.)

I MUST WARN YOU I'M A KARATE EXPERT AND I DON'T WANT TO HURT YOU.

HOLD ME BACK OR I'LL KILL HIM.
(I said someone hold me back . . . please.)

Admit defeat, and then hit him from behind.

F

F I S H I N G

Never use this clichéd piece of bullshit:

YOU SHOULD HAVE SEEN THE ONE THAT GOT AWAY.

Here are some that are more believable:

If you come across a beached whale, quickly place your hook in its mouth then turn and say to any people who have gathered, 'Excuse me, would someone give me a hand to throw this one back.'

Go to a fish market and purchase a 100kg tuna and tell them you are using it as bait. Make sure you unwrap it before you get home.

THEY WERE TOO BIG TO PULL INTO THE BOAT.

I NEVER GET SEASICK.

I LET IT GO BECAUSE IT THREATENED TO CAPSIZE THE BOAT.

MATE – NO BULLSHIT – IT WAS THIS BIG.
(Just use one hand.)

I CAUGHT HEAPS OF FISH. TAG AND RELEASE IS MY METHOD. I HAD TO COME IN, THOUGH, AS I RAN OUT OF TAGS.

MATE, IT WAS THAT BIG THE PHOTO WEIGHED FOUR KILOS.

F LY I N G

Passengers
OH, DON'T WORRY, I'VE FLOWN HUNDREDS OF TIMES AND
I'VE NEVER HAD ANY PROBLEMS.
(If you follow this comment with uncontrollable sobbing
and constant referrals to death and life insurance it may
cast some doubt on your sincerity.)

Pilots
I'M JUST STEPPING OUT FOR A WHILE.
(Say this casually so as not to cause panic.)

Flight attendant
DON'T WORRY, SIR, IT'S QUITE NORMAL FOR A PLANE TO
NOSEDIVE WHEN IT LOSES A WING.

Is there a doctor or a pilot on the plane who didn't eat the chicken?

WE'VE LOST OUR CLOCK. IF YOU CAN HEAR IT TICKING COULD YOU PLEASE RAISE YOUR HAND?
(Gently.)

DOES ANYONE KNOW HOW TO FLY A 747?

WE KNOW WHERE YOUR LUGGAGE IS.
(On another plane heading in the opposite direction.)

DID YOU ENJOY YOUR MEAL?
(Sure, that's why I'm buckled over.)

When all hope is gone:

PLEASE DISCARD ANY FLAMMABLE CLOTHING. IF YOU REACH UNDER YOUR SEAT YOU'LL FIND AN INDIVIDUALLY WRAPPED BODY BAG – COULD YOU KINDLY SLIP IT ON.

Flypaper

G O D

Lying to God on Judgement Day
WELL, I WAS GOING TO REPENT. I WAS ON MY WAY TO
CONFESSION THIS AFTERNOON WHEN I WAS HIT BY A
BUS.

God telling lies
I MADE THE WORLD IN SIX DAYS.

I LOVE MANKIND.

LISTEN TO THE POPE.

YOU'RE ALL GOING TO HEAVEN.

G R A N D P A R E N T S

Top bum crawler lies to get into the will
I LOVE YOU.
(What you leave me is irrelevant but the BMW will need to be registered.)

YOU MEAN THE WORLD TO ME.
(Your money will do me the world of good.)

YOU DON'T SMELL LIKE MOTHBALLS.
(Rancid mincemeat, perhaps.)

Receiving presents
WOW – OLD SPICE – JUST WHAT I WANTED!

WOW – BIG WHITE UNDIES – JUST WHAT I WANTED!

Getting the inheritance

COME OVER TO THE EDGE OF THE CLIFF – I WON'T PUSH YOU.

COME ON, CROSS THE ROAD, YOU'LL MAKE IT.

Grandparents lying

I DON'T HAVE ALZHEIMER'S.
(Who are you anyway?)

GROUPIES

What to say to security to get backstage at concerts:

IT'S OBVIOUS YOU DON'T KNOW WHO I AM.

SORRY I'M LATE, HAVE THEY BEEN ASKING FOR ME?

WHAT DO YOU MEAN MY NAME ISN'T ON THE BACKSTAGE
LIST?
(When they pull it out to check, spot someone else's name
and say, 'There it is – they must have used my stage name
instead.')

Face lift

H OUSE G UESTS

The old unwanted house guests – don't they piss you off? When you want them to leave:

BUY THEM LUGGAGE OR A TRAVEL KIT.

WATCH MOVIES WITH AN APPROPRIATE THEME, E.G. *HOME ALONE*.

PLAY SONGS WITH AN APPROPRIATE THEME, E.G. 'LEAVING ON A JET PLANE'.

If hints don't work, try a more direct approach:

GEE – IF YOU DIDN'T EAT ALL OUR FOOD, DRINK ALL OUR ALCOHOL AND ACT LIKE A PIG, I'D ASK YOU TO STAY OVER A LITTLE LONGER.

ISN'T IT TIME YOU PISSED OFF?
(Not a lie but really effective.)

SORRY, I'M GOING TO HAVE TO ASK YOU TO LEAVE AS MY
PSYCHIATRIST WILL BE HERE ANY MOMENT TO TAKE ME TO
MY NEW CRIMINALLY INSANE WARD.

OH, ARE YOU STILL HERE? I THOUGHT YOU LEFT AGES AGO.

GEE – IS IT THAT TIME ALREADY?
(Just start yawning at them.)

I WISH WE COULD INVITE YOU IN BUT WE WERE JUST
LEAVING OURSELVES.

H

H O U S E W O R K

I'VE DONE IT.

WELL, I'VE JUST DONE IT A COUPLE OF DAYS AGO.

I DON'T USE THE TOILET.

I'VE BEEN WORKING MY FINGERS TO THE BONE.
(Works well if you're a thalidomide victim or have arthritis.)

I ALWAYS PUT OUT THE GARBAGE.
(Put it out all the way through the house.)

I DID THE WASHING-UP YESTERDAY.
(Yeah, that's why it's piled to the roof.)

I HAVEN'T WASHED UP BECAUSE I'M TRYING TO SAVE WATER.
(That must be the same reason for you not having a shower this year.)

I'M USING THE SINK FOR PENICILLIN RESEARCH.

THAT'S NOT SHAGPILE CARPET, IT'S THE LINO.

THERE'S NO POINT CLEANING IT, WE'LL BE OUT OF HERE SOON – THE LEASE IS UP IN SIX MONTHS.

I'M GOING FOR THE LIVED-IN LOOK.

I'VE GOT A DISHWASHER.
(But he's too busy vacuuming at the moment.)

I'LL DO IT TOMORROW.

Black eye

INTRODUCTIONS

Isn't it the worst when you go to introduce someone and forget their name? Here are some handy hints:

JUST EVERYONE INTRODUCE THEMSELVES. I'VE GOT TO GO TO THE TOILET.

When meeting someone who obviously knows you and you can't remember them, start fishing for clues.

SO WHAT HAVE YOU BEEN DOING LATELY?

WHERE HAVE YOU BEEN GOING OUT?

HOW'S WORK?
(Doesn't work on the unemployed, but then who cares anyway?)

WHAT'S YOUR NAME AGAIN?
(Ask them their name and when they tell you, say, 'I know your first name, silly, I mean your second name!')

HAVEN'T I SEEN YOU SOMEWHERE BEFORE?
(Perhaps on a 'Wanted' poster.)

If all else fails, wait until someone comes up and introduces themselves.

Heart attack

J

J O B S

Some useful lies for job interviews:

OH – THAT'S A PIECE OF CAKE.
(Don't point to the interviewer's morning tea or use if applying for a job in a bakery.)

I'VE NEVER TAKEN A SICK DAY AND I DON'T INTEND TO.
(Because I've never had a job.)

I'M AN EXTREMELY HARD WORKER.
(Don't use this if applying for a civil servant's job or yawning.)

I'M THE MAN FOR THE JOB.
(Don't say this wearing a skirt.)

I COULD DO IT STANDING ON MY HEAD.
(Use this when applying for a job as an acrobat.)

YOU CAN BANK ON ME.
(A teller.)

I'M GOOD AT BOOKKEEPING.
(I've been out at the races every day this week.)

I'M GOOD WITH FIGURES.
(36, 24, 36)

I CAN SPEAK FIVE DIFFERENT LANGUAGES.
(American, English, Australian, Canadian, New Zealand.)

I BELIEVE THE JOB WOULD BE BOTH CHALLENGING AND REWARDING.

Kitty litter

KIDDING YOURSELF

I SUPPOSE I COULD LOSE A FEW POUNDS.
(A few? Who are you kidding – you're a planet. When you walk into the lounge the furniture goes into orbit around you. You even have your own moon. If you died tomorrow they would have to bury you in a mass grave.)

I THINK I'VE JUST PUT ON A FEW POUNDS.
(A few? Who are you kidding – you're a walking chicken wing. You have to jump up and down on the bathroom scales to get a reading.)

I'M NOT GOING BALD. I JUST HAVE A HIGH FOREHEAD.
(Who are you kidding? Your hairline is between your shoulder blades. There is as much chance of hair growing

on your head as there is of harvesting a wheat crop on the moon.)

I THINK I MIGHT GET LAID TONIGHT.
(Listen, you've got more chance of winning the lottery without buying a ticket.)

CAN I HAVE A PACKET OF EXTRA LARGE CONDOMS, PLEASE?

I'M REALLY POPULAR.

I'M GOING TO GET A JOB TOMORROW.

THESE THONGS ARE REALLY SEXY.

SHE REALLY LOVES ME, SHE'S JUST PLAYING HARD TO GET.

I'VE GOT AIDS, BUT I'LL GET OVER IT.

I THINK I'LL JUST HAVE ONE MORE.

K

KIDS

THAT IS GOING TO HURT ME MORE THAN IT HURTS YOU. (The child may be a little sceptical if you say this while wearing a party hat, singing 'Happy days are here again'.)

For nagging children who pester you with 'Can I please, mummy, can I, can I, can I?':

ASK YOUR FATHER.

I'LL THINK ABOUT IT.

NO.

With children, if you want them to do something just tell them *not* to do it. You can bet your life they will do it as soon as your back's turned. Some good ones to try are:

WHATEVER YOU DO, DON'T GO AND STICK THIS CHEWING GUM IN MUMMY'S HAIR WHILE SHE'S SLEEPING.

DON'T SHAKE DADDY'S BEER IN THE FRIDGE JUST BEFORE HE OPENS IT.

To take revenge on a nagging child, try the following:

DON'T TOUCH DADDY'S GUN.

Breast implants

LANDLORD

Lies to tell the landlord:

I'VE GOT NO IDEA HOW THE HOUSE CAUGHT ON FIRE.
(Never use this while holding a can of petrol.)

THOSE STAINS WERE ON THE CARPET WHEN I MOVED IN.

To hide the stain:
* Put a couch over it.
* Stand on the stains when they come to inspect it.
* Make the same stain all over the carpet so as to make
  it look like a pattern on the carpet.

NO, WE DON'T HAVE ANY ANIMALS.
(This won't work if you live on a farm.)

I'LL PAY THE RENT FIRST THING IN THE MORNING.
(Works well if you live in Antarctica where they have eight-month nights.)

COME IN, THE PIT BULL TERRIERS DON'T BITE.

THE PLACE WAS A DUMP WHEN I MOVED IN.
(Don't use this if you have leased the local tip.)

LIE DETECTORS

TRUE.
(False.)

FALSE.
(True.)

I DON'T KNOW.
(I know.)

I KNOW.
(I don't know what you're talking about.)

L O V E R S

Refusing sex for women

I'M SORRY, DARLING, I DON'T KNOW WHAT'S WRONG WITH ME TONIGHT. I USUALLY FIND YOUR CLUMSY FOREPLAY AND THE SIGHT OF YOUR HUGE BULBOUS GUT AND BRIGHT RED FACE CONTORTED IN PLEASURE AS YOU BELCH AND FART YOUR WAY TOWARDS A CLIMAX IRRESISTIBLE. PERHAPS I NEED COUNSELLING.

Refusing sex for men

Ending relationships

I THINK WE NEED SPACE.

(How much? The other side of the planet should do it.)

CAN WE JUST BE FRIENDS?
(Why? We weren't while we were dating.)

Here are some brownie lies to suck your partner in.
Try to keep a straight face.

I LOVE YOU.
(Shit, yeah.)

YOU'RE THE ONLY ONE FOR ME.
(You're the only one I can get.)

OF COURSE I RESPECT YOU.
(Who are you?)

YOU'RE GREAT AT SEX.
(Have you started? Oh – you've finished.)

YOU'RE GREAT AT SEX.
(A nice thing to say especially if you're alone.)

I THINK YOU'RE SO BEAUTIFUL.
(Your face is a work of art – a Picasso.)

OH, I'M COMING.
(You've never had one in your life, and probably never
will.)

NO, I HAVEN'T COME YET.
(Since I took your pants off, anyway.)

OF COURSE YOU'RE NOT FAT.
(But who hit you in the back of your legs with a
shotgun?)

Note: While in bed, give your partner a headache tablet.
When they say 'But I haven't got a headache', they'll have
no excuse for refusing sex.

Sleeping pill

M A S T U R B A T I N G

Lies to use if sprung:

I WAS JUST TRYING TO GET THE WRINKLES OUT OF IT.

I WAS JUST RUBBING IT TO KEEP IT WARM.

I WAS JUST TRYING TO GET MY TAMPON OUT, WITH MY DILDO.

I WAS JUST TRYING TO TAKE THE SWELLING OUT OF IT.

WHAT BROOM HANDLE?

I WAS JUST TAKING A PISS.
(Don't say this if you're standing in the lounge.)

I'VE JUST JOINED THE IN VITRO FERTILISATION PROGRAMME AND THEY'VE ASKED FOR A DONATION.

I'VE JUST STARTED WORK AT A SPERM BANK AND I'M DOING A LITTLE OVERTIME.

I WAS THINKING OF YOU.
(Not a good one if one of your parents catches you.)

I WAS JUST CLEANING IT.
(With my mouth.)

M

MECHANICS

Watch out for mechanics because if you are not mechanically minded they will come out with some real bullshit to rip you off.
Lies your mechanic will use:

THE REASON YOUR BLINKER WASN'T WORKING WAS BECAUSE THE MANIFOLD IN THE CARBURETTOR WASN'T IN RATIO WITH THE DIFFERENTIAL SUMP EXHAUST REGULATOR – THAT WILL BE £500.

SORRY, WE'RE STILL WAITING ON THE PART TO COME IN. (Standard lie – they really haven't even looked at it yet. And even if it doesn't need the part they will charge you for it anyway.)

I'M SORRY, WE JUST CAN'T SEEM TO GET THESE ROUND

THINGS TO MOVE.
(If he's talking about the wheels, leave in a hurry.)

IT SHOULD BE READY FIRST THING IN THE MORNING.
(Yeah, which morning?)

M

M O B I L E   P H O N E S

Get wake-up calls set for every five minutes so when you're in a restaurant you seem to be really popular. Some lines to use when talking in public on your mobile phone:

LISTEN . . . I DON'T CARE HOW MUCH THEY COST . . . JUST BUY 100,000 OF THEM NOW.

MEL GIBSON . . . HOW ARE YOU? . . . LISTEN, MATE, I'LL TALK TO YOU LATER ABOUT MY NEW FILM.

MADONNA . . . I'D LOVE TO FLY OVER AND HAVE LUNCH WITH YOU.

WHAT DO YOU MEAN MY THREE GOLD PORSCHES HAVEN'T ARRIVED?

YEAH, LISTEN, I'M THINKING OF BUYING THE OPERA HOUSE.

ELVIS . . . I TOLD YOU NOT TO RING ME ON THIS NUMBER.

YOUR MAJESTY . . . HOW DID YOU KNOW IT WAS MY BIRTHDAY?

M

MONEY

CAN YOU LEND ME £20 – I'LL PAY YOU BACK TOMORROW.

I PAID YOU THAT MONEY BACK AGES AGO.
(Don't use this the next day after borrowing the money.)

DO YOU TAKE CHEQUES?
(Sure, but not from you.)

WHAT ABOUT A RAIN CHECK ON THE MONEY I OWE YOU?

I KNOW I'M ONLY 20 YEARS OLD, BUT I'M ATTRACTED TO
SIR MONTY JAMES BECAUSE MEN OVER 100 ARE VERY
ATTRACTIVE AND STIMULATING, NOT BECAUSE HE'S A
BILLIONAIRE WITH NO CLOSE RELATIVES.

I FOUND IT.
(In your wallet.)

I HAVEN'T SEEN YOUR MONEY.
(Since I spent it.)

HONEY, I NEED SOME MONEY TO PAY ALL THESE BILLS.
(Beauty salon, Tiffany's, David Jones, Pierre Cardin – the necessities of life aren't cheap, you know.)

M

M O T H E R - I N - L A W

YOU'RE LOOKING BEAUTIFUL TODAY.

I WISH YOU COULD STAY OVER THIS WEEKEND, BUT WE
HAVE OTHER FRIENDS COMING OVER SOON, SO BEST YOU
LEAVE NOW.

WE'VE BEEN TRYING TO RING YOU BUT NO ONE HAS BEEN
ANSWERING.

GEE, YOUR HAIR IS LOOKING GREAT TODAY. IS THAT ITS
NATURAL COLOUR – PURPLE?

DIDN'T WE TELL YOU THAT WE MOVED?

LET'S GO BUNGEE JUMPING – YOU'LL BE ALL RIGHT. OF
COURSE I'VE TIED THE ROPE ON PROPERLY.

YOU LOOK LIKE MARILYN MONROE.
(After she died.)

NO, I'M NOT IGNORING YOU – I WAS JUST THINKING OF SOMETHING ELSE.
(Yeah, where to hide the body.)

IS THAT A NEW PERFUME OR HAVE YOU JUST WASHED OFF THE OLD STUFF?

If your mother-in-law arrives at your front door and asks 'Can I stay here for a fortnight?', say 'Yes', then close the door on her and scream through the door: 'You can stay there for as long as you like.'

M

MURDER

HE LUNGED AT ME WHILE I WAS HOLDING THE KNIFE.
(Thirty times.)

I DIDN'T KNOW THE GUN WAS LOADED.
(Because I had already put six rounds into him.)

Tell them the truth and they will never believe you.

I HAVEN'T SEEN MY WIFE FOR A WHILE BECAUSE I'VE
KILLED HER. AS A MATTER OF FACT I'M JUST ABOUT TO DIG
THE GRAVE NOW. DO YOU THINK YOU COULD GIVE ME A
HAND WITH THE BODY?

Sleeping bag

NEIGHBOURS

I'M GOING ON HOLIDAY FOR A LONG TIME SO DON'T BOTHER KNOCKING.

THAT WASN'T MY STEREO TURNED UP LAST NIGHT.
(But there was a heavy metal band playing in our lounge.)

ALL THAT SCREAMING YOU HEARD LAST NIGHT WAS A HORROR MOVIE WE WERE WATCHING.
(Don't explain this while digging a grave in your back yard.)

I DON'T KNOW WHO RAN OVER YOUR DOG LAST NIGHT.

DO YOU KNOW WHO SET YOUR HOUSE ON FIRE?
(Make sure the 'Little Lucifers' packet is out of sight and not hanging out of your back pocket.)

Nuclear Testing

WHAT'S A LITTLE NUCLEAR TEST?

WE ARE VERY CONSERVATION MINDED.
(A little atomic explosion will have two-headed people
running around everywhere, therefore increasing the head
count without the resource problem of extra bodies.)

IT'S NECESSARY.

Titsy fly

OLD PEOPLE

WE'LL COME AND VISIT YOU AGAIN SOON.
(Around the turn of the century.)

OF COURSE YOU'RE NOT A BURDEN TO THE NATIONAL
HEALTH SERVICE – A HEARING AID, GLASSES, A
COLOSTOMY BAG, A WALKING FRAME, A PACEMAKER,
FALSE TEETH, A TOUPEE, A RESPIRATOR – YOU REALLY ARE A
PICTURE OF HEALTH.

Lies old people will tell you:

I'M MIDDLE AGED.
(Sure, if you were going to live until you were 240.)

I MAY BE OLD BUT I DO HAVE WISDOM.
(This comment is invalid if they say it sitting at a poker

machine dribbling into a beer tankard.)

On losing their looks:

YEAH, THE YEARS HAVE BEEN REALLY GOOD TO YOU.
(This will obviously be bullshit if the person you're talking
to resembles a prune wearing a toupee.)

YOU DON'T LOOK A DAY OLDER.
(. . . Than the pyramids.)

DON'T WORRY – I THINK CROW'S FEET, A TURKEY NECK
AND JOWLS ARE A REALLY GOOD LOOK!

OF COURSE YOU'RE NOT UGLY, YOU'RE JUST VISUALLY
CHALLENGING.

ONE-NIGHT STANDS

HURRY UP AND GET DRESSED – I'M LATE FOR WORK.
(Works well if you have a job.)

QUICK – HURRY UP AND GET OUT OF HERE. MY
HUSBAND'S COMING.
(If you're female, keep a photo next to your bed of a Hell's
Angel. Show the picture ten seconds before telling the
above line. It works much better.)

RUN OUT THE BACK DOOR. I'LL KEEP HIM AT BAY FOR A
WHILE.
(Have a pre-taped voice of your partner on a tape recorder
– screaming, 'Let me in, I know you're in there.' Turn it
on while returning from the bathroom.)

LEAVE ME YOUR NUMBER AND I'LL CALL YOU.
(Shit, yeah.)

I THINK I LOVE YOU.
(This line will scare away 99 per cent of people in an instant. Warning – do beware of the torrid 1 per cent.)

AH OH.
(Violently scratch your crotch every 20 seconds. This is sure to piss 'em off – one of my personal favourites.)

I PROBABLY WON'T SEE YOU AGAIN AS I'M LEAVING FOR ALASKA TODAY.
(Don't say this to an Eskimo.)

ORGASMING

The funny thing about orgasming is that guys fake not having them and girls fake having them.

OH YEAH, OH YEAH, OH YEAH, BABY, THAT FEELS SO GOOD.
(Make sure you're in the same room.)

If you have faked an orgasm, a good thing to do is light up a cigarette. This is standard procedure after orgasming.

For a bloke, if you faked *not* having one do not go straight to sleep – this is an obvious bust.

If you pre-ejaculate, roll off screaming, and blame it on a cramp. This will give you enough time to reload.

Try not to scream out someone else's name.

Definite nos:
* Oh Mr Postman
* Oh Mr Milkman
* Oh Mr Garbologist
* Oh Fat Cat

Definitely do not scream out your own name.

'OH, I'M COMING.'
(Don't scream this while purchasing your condoms.)

Premature ejaculation
I'M SORRY, DARLING, I COULDN'T CONTROL MYSELF.
(Don't say this while having dinner.)

IF ONLY YOU WEREN'T SO DAMNED ATTRACTIVE.

Just after you ejaculate, reach over and turn forward your clock by 45 minutes and say: 'Doesn't time fly when you're having fun?'

Be as boring in bed as you can, so that 45 seconds will feel like an eternity.

For Australians only:
Don't give a shit, roll over and go to sleep.

Blame them.

Tell them it's their fault because they're more beautiful than the stars on a midsummer night's stroll and a ravishing sex machine to boot.

Block of flats

PARKING

I ONLY PARKED HERE FIVE MINUTES AGO.
(This will not work if you're parked in the middle of a three-lane carriageway.)

THE PARKING METER IS BROKEN.
(If they put a coin in and it works, say: 'Would you look at that. It's working again!')

WHERE ARE THE TRAFFIC WARDENS?

I THINK YOU'RE DOING A REALLY GOOD JOB.
(Now I've sold my car.)

I'M PARKED IN THE DISABLED SECTION BECAUSE I'M FROM THE COUNTRY.
(Try and look stupid.)

Another good one is when you walk up, act like a spastic. Most people won't even have to act.

SORRY FOR RUNNING YOU OVER. I DIDN'T SEE YOU STANDING IN FRONT OF MY CAR BOOKING ME.
(Note: If you do the job properly you won't have to say this.)

WHERE CAN I SIGN UP TO BE A TRAFFIC WARDEN, BECAUSE I RECKON ALL YOUSE BLOKES ARE GROUSE.

If you park in a no-waiting zone, put a broken-down sign on your car. Most of the time this will baffle them. DO NOT leave the engine running.

P

P E T S

COME HERE, COME ON BOY, COME HERE. I'M NOT GOING
TO HIT YOU JUST BECAUSE YOU CHEWED UP MY BEST
TROUSERS AND SHIT ALL OVER THE KITCHEN FLOOR AND
HUMPED MY LEG FOR THREE HOURS WHILE I WAS TRYING
TO SLEEP.
(Use this with a soft tone of voice so as not to scare him.)

Putting your dog down
COME ON, ROVER, IT'S TIME FOR YOUR DISTEMPER SHOTS.

Things to avoid while going on the final ride:
* Don't slow down while driving past a pet cemetery.
* Hide the 'For Sale' sign on the kennel.
* Don't offer the dog a cigarette and a blindfold prior to
  the injection.
* Don't look at the cat and give it the thumbs up.

* Don't remove the dog's tags and say, 'Well, you won't
 be needing these any more.'

P

PICK-UP LINES

Pick-up lines guaranteed to fail:

HI – MY NAME'S RASH.

HI – I'M A FRIEND OF RASH'S.

HI – AREN'T YOU RASH'S FRIEND?

WHERE HAVE YOU BEEN ALL MY LIFE?
(Prison.)

WHERE HAVE YOU BEEN ALL YOUR LIFE?

WOULD YOU HAVE A LIGHT, PLEASE?
(Don't use this if you're in an oxygen tent.)

HAVEN'T I SEEN YOU SOMEWHERE BEFORE?
(This line doesn't apply to Elvis, the Queen or Siamese twins.)

HOW ABOUT WE GO FOR A RIDE IN MY LAMBORGHINI?
(Walk outside until you find a vacant car space and say, 'Oh, someone must have stolen it.' Also, you will get some sympathy from them.)

HAS ANYONE EVER TOLD YOU THAT YOU HAVE THE MOST BEAUTIFUL EYE?
(Only works with Cyclops.)

DO YOU BELIEVE IN LOVE AT FIRST SIGHT?
(Make sure they're not blind.)

DO YOU BELIEVE IN CONTEMPT AT FIRST SIGHT?

WOULD YOU CARE TO COME BACK TO MY PLACE? I HAVE OVALTINE AND DIGESTIVE BISCUITS.

WHAT'S A GLAMOROUS PERSON LIKE YOURSELF DOING IN A PLACE LIKE THIS?

P

POLICE

I DON'T KNOW WHAT YOU'RE TALKING ABOUT.
(Make sure you've taken care of your balaclava.)

IT WASN'T ME.
(He just looks like me and has the same name.)

HOW COULD I HAVE DONE IT? I'VE ONLY BEEN OUT OF
PRISON FOR HALF AN HOUR.

I'VE GOT NO IDEA HOW THAT TELEVISION AND VIDEO
RECORDER GOT IN THE BOOT OF MY CAR. IN FACT, IT'S
NOT EVEN MY CAR. I FOUND IT IN THE GUTTER AND I WAS
ON MY WAY TO THE STATION TO REPORT IS AS 'FOUND'.

WHAT DEAD BODY?
(This would be a good time to get rid of the gun.)

I'VE NEVER SEEN THAT PERSON BEFORE IN MY LIFE.
(Make sure it's not your Siamese twin.)

BLIMEY – AM I GLAD TO SEE YOU, OFFICERS.
(Not really effective if they're bashing you with their truncheons.)

THANKS, OFFICER, I WILL NEVER DO IT AGAIN.
(Make sure you're not bashing them with a truncheon.)

I WAS JUST STANDING THERE MINDING MY OWN BUSINESS WHEN THESE DOBERMANNS ATTACKED ME.
(Helps if you're off the person's property and doesn't really work too well when you're in someone else's bedroom.)

BOY – HOW DID THAT £10 NOTE GET WRAPPED AROUND MY LICENCE?
(I thought it was a £20 note.)

SORRY, I PROMISE I WILL NEVER DO IT AGAIN, OFFICER.
(Make sure you haven't shot his partner.)

In response to:
Would you mind coming to the station with us, please?

IT'S OKAY, OFFICER, I'LL CATCH A CAB.

I'd like to see your licence.

SO WOULD I!

P

Do you have a criminal record?

YES, THE ALBUM COMES OUT LATER IN THE YEAR.

P O L I T I C I A N S

Let's face it – where do we start here!

BY THE YEAR 2000, THERE WILL BE NO HOMELESS PEOPLE IN BRITAIN.

WE WILL STOP UNEMPLOYMENT.

THERE WILL BE NO MORE HOSPITAL WAITING LISTS.

NO POLICE WILL TAKE BRIBES.

INCOME TAXES WILL GO DOWN.

I AM TELLING THE TRUTH.

WE PROMISE MORE HOSPITALS.

WE PROMISE MORE HELP FOR THE MENTALLY
HANDICAPPED.

P S Y C H I A T R I S T S

Lying to a sociopath
OF COURSE YOU'LL FIND A GIRLFRIEND ONE DAY. MOST WOMEN FIND MANICALLY DEPRESSED, PARANOID PSYCHOPATHS WITH SUICIDAL AND HOMICIDAL TENDENCIES HIGHLY ATTRACTIVE.

Lying to the psychiatrist
I AM NOT MAD.
(No, of course not. That's why you're here.)

SO, YOU THINK YOU'RE A TEASPOON?
(Well, sit there and don't stir.)

SO, YOU THINK YOU'RE A GUITAR?
(Well, sit there and don't fret.)

P

SO, YOU THINK YOU'RE A CASHEW?
(That doesn't mean you're nuts.)

THE PUB

I'VE BEEN WITH HER.

I CAN MAKE MINE 12 INCHES LONG BY BENDING IT IN HALF.

LEND ME SOME MONEY. I'LL PAY YOU BACK FIRST THING IN THE MORNING.
(Because I'm that blind drunk I won't wake up until late afternoon.)

I CAN DO THAT HEAPS BETTER THAN YOU.
(Anything you can do I can do better.)

LISTEN TO ME. I'LL TELL YOU HOW GOOD I AM.
(Pissed wanker.)

BUY US A DRINK, WILL YOU? I FORGOT MY WALLET.
(Again.)

A FEW BEERS NEVER HURT ANYONE.
(Just ask the Kidney and Liver Foundation.)

I TOLD THAT BITCH AT HOME, I SAID, LISTEN, BITCH. I'M
GOING DOWN TO THE PUB TO GET PISSED WITH THE
BOYS WHETHER YOU LIKE IT OR NOT.
(In fact: 'Honey, sweety, sugar lips, please, oh pretty
please, could you find it in your most precious heart to let
me go down to the hotel for just one shandy, please?')

Hyde park

T H E   Q U E E N

WE DON'T REALLY WANT TO BECOME A REPUBLIC.

IS IT POSSIBLE TO BE AWARDED AN MBE FOR BRICKIE'S LABOURING?

THE MONEY SPENT ON YOU IS WORTH EVERY PENNY.

HERE ARE MY CROWN JEWELS.

Killer whale

REAL ESTATE

AN IDEAL FIRST INVESTMENT!
(This means whatever you do, don't live in this dump yourself.)

CLOSE TO ALL TRANSPORT.
(It means it's on a flight path, or a railway station detours through your garden.)

ELEGANT VICTORIAN STYLE.
(Means it's a ruin, ready for demolition.)

COSY.
(Means it's a shoebox – the owner was Old Mother Hubbard.)

SPECTACULAR VIEW.
(Yeah, if you like a brick wall.)

NEEDS A LITTLE TLC.
(And a £100,000 renovation.)

HAS A SUNNY OUTLOOK.
(Needs a whole new roof.)

R

RELIGION

Confession
SORRY, GOD, FOR KILLING 30 PEOPLE THIS WEEK. I WON'T
DO IT AGAIN.

Next week
SORRY, GOD, FOR KILLING ANOTHER 30 PEOPLE THIS WEEK.
I WON'T DO IT AGAIN.

If Mormons come to your door:
Answer it in the nude, preferably with a knife in your
hand.

Draw an outline of a dead body on the pathway to your
front door.

If Jehovah's Witnesses come to your door:
COME IN – WE'RE JUST ABOUT TO SACRIFICE A GOAT.

Say that you're a Mormon and ask for *their* address.

DO I KNOW ABOUT THE 'WATCH TOWER'? YEAH, I SPENT
SIX HOURS THERE LAST NIGHT.

Ask them if they actually witnessed Jehovah, and when
they say no, call them fakes and liars and throw them
out.

R

R ESTAURANTS

How to skip the queue
I PERSONALLY MADE THE RESERVATIONS MYSELF.
(Don't use this in KFC or McDonald's.)

I WANT A TABLE NOW. IT'S OBVIOUS THAT YOU DON'T
KNOW WHO WE ARE.
(This will really have the waiters baffled. The rest of the
day they will be saying – 'Who is that?')

Free meals
Stuff a pillow up your girlfriend's dress so she looks
pregnant. Just as you have nearly finished your meal, tip
some tomato sauce on her thighs. Get her to scream,
'Oh, my God, it's coming.' Grab her hand and rush from
the restaurant.

If you spill soup on your lap
EXCUSE ME, WAITER – THERE'S A SOUP IN MY FLY.

If the service is slow
EXCUSE ME, WAITER – I DIDN'T REALISE THIS WAS A BUFFET.

After-dinner abuse
COMPLIMENTS TO THE CHEF – TELL HIM HE'S CHARMING, INTELLIGENT AND GOOD LOOKING, BUT THAT HE CAN'T COOK FOR SHIT.

Ordering
Impress your date – order your meals in French.

BONJOUR GARÇON, DEUX LE BIG MACS, DEUX LE THICK SHAKES AND LE FRENCH FRIES, S'IL VOUS PLAÎT.

Laughing stock

S ALESMEN

To be a good salesman you must be a blatant liar, obey the Ten Commandments (as stated in the front of this book) and be a chameleon – depending on the situation. Here are a few beauties.

YEAH, THEY ALWAYS DO THAT, THAT'S STANDARD.

THAT MARK WILL COME OFF.

IT ALWAYS SOUNDS LIKE THAT.

THE BOAT IS RUNNING LATE.

THEY ARE STUCK IN CUSTOMS.

IT MUST BE LOST IN THE POST!

THE SHIPMENT WAS STOLEN.

THE CONTAINER FELL OFF THE BOAT.

THEY ARE STILL STUCK IN CUSTOMS.

THEY SENT IT TO OUR OTHER OFFICE, THE DUMMIES.

IT'LL BE THERE TOMORROW.

YOU SHOULD GET IT TODAY.

I PUT IT ON THE TRUCK MYSELF.

YEAH, 100 PER CENT GUARANTEE.

NO PROBLEM, GOOD AS GOLD.

FUNNY, YOU ARE THE FIRST ONE TO COMPLAIN.

I'VE GOT ONE MYSELF, THEY ARE GREAT.

MY GIRLFRIEND'S GOT THE SAME ONE, SHE LOVES IT.

MY OLD MAN'S HAD ONE FOR YEARS, SWEARS BY IT.

THAT LOOKS GREAT ON YOU.

NO, THEY DON'T RUST, BUCKLE, BEND OR BUST.

YES, VERY EASY TO HOUSE-TRAIN.

IT'S A QUIET NEIGHBOURHOOD, REALLY.

IT'S JUST LIKE A NEW ONE.

IT'S A BARGAIN.

NO, MADAM/SIR, THIS IS STATE-OF-THE-ART STUFF.

YES, THAT IS THE DISCOUNT PRICE.

THAT IS YOU!

SARCASM

IF YOU EVER HAVE A NOSE JOB THEY COULD BUILD
ANOTHER PERSON WITH WHAT THEY TAKE OFF.

YOUR PENIS IS SO SMALL YOU COULD ALWAYS USE YOUR
NOSE INSTEAD.

IF YOU WRAP SILVER FOIL AROUND YOUR EARS, YOU'D BE
SOLAR POWERED.

GEE, I LIKE YOUR HAIRCUT . . . DID YOU DO IT YOURSELF?

GEE, I LIKE YOUR NEW HAIRCUT . . . WHEN DO YOU THINK
YOU'LL BE ABLE TO GO OUT IN PUBLIC AGAIN?

THAT'S A GREAT SHIRT. WHERE DID YOU GET IT?
(Market stall.)

WOW, I LIKE YOUR CAR.
(Is it registered?)

MMM . . . THIS DINNER TASTES GREAT.
(Did you boil these hamburgers yourself?)

BOY, I LOVE THAT NEW FRENCH PERFUME YOU'RE
WEARING.
(Or have you shit yourself?)

NICE HAT.
(I think brown paper really suits you.)

LOVE YOUR ACCENT.
(Works well on Aussies.)

GEE, HAVE YOU LOST SOME WEIGHT?
(It looks like it because I can get around you now.)

GEE, I WISH I HAD YOUR LOOKS.
(So I had a decent reason to kill myself.)

CAN YOU BREATHE ON ME A LITTLE HARDER?
(Because I love the smell of garlic.)

GEE, YOU'VE GOT A GREAT SMILE.
(Too bad we can see your teeth.)

I NEVER NOTICED YOU HAD SIX-INCH-THICK HAIR ON
YOUR BACK. IT FEELS GREAT.
(To an ape.)

YOU LOOK FANTASTIC IN THE NUDE.
(When the light's off.)

I THINK BALD MEN ARE REALLY SEXY.
(Except when they've got hair growing out of their ears.
But don't worry, they match the ones coming out of your
nose.)

I'M SO ENVIOUS OF YOUR JOB.
(Because if I had it that would give me a good reason to
go on the dole.)

DID YOU GET A PROFESSIONAL MAKE-UP ARTIST TO PUT
YOUR MAKE-UP ON?
(Yes, Bozo the clown.)

YOU LOOK BEAUTIFUL TONIGHT.
(Thank God it's dark.)

Presents

JUST WHAT I ALWAYS WANTED.
(A toilet brush with my initials on it.)

IT'S GREAT. I LOVE IT.
(What is it?)

S E X

I'M CELIBATE.
(Biggest joke of the year.)

IT DOESN'T MATTER HOW BIG IT IS, IT'S HOW YOU USE IT.
(If you use this one everyone will know you are not well endowed.)

I'M NOT VERY EXPERIENCED AT THIS.

COULD YOU TEACH ME HOW TO MAKE LOVE?
(Concentrate. You'll only have three seconds to learn in.)

DON'T – OH, STOP IT.
(As they're undressing themselves.)

YOU'RE THE BEST LOVER I'VE EVER HAD.
(Did I tell you I was a virgin?)

I'VE NEVER DONE THIS BEFORE.
(Not to be used by prostitutes.)

Shoplifting

HOW THE HELL DID ALL THOSE GROCERIES GET INTO MY BAG?
(Don't say this if you're still putting them in.)

I JUST WANT TO SEE IT IN THE SUNLIGHT.
(Make sure it's not raining or night time.)

I BROUGHT THIS REFRIGERATOR WITH ME.

I WAS EATING THE BISCUITS TO MAKE SURE THEY WEREN'T STALE.

I THOUGHT THEY WERE SAMPLES.

I FORGOT I HAD THE TELEVISION UNDER MY ARM.

I'M GOING TO PAY FOR IT.
(Yeah, in about three years.)

DON'T WORRY – I OWN THE STORE.
(Don't say this to the owner.)

SORRY, I WAS JUST HELPING YOU GET RID OF SOME OF THIS
OLD STOCK.
(Don't use this in an antique shop.)

SOCIAL SECURITY

NO, I HAVEN'T GOT ANOTHER JOB.
(Don't go with your McDonald's outfit on and especially don't ask them if they want fries with that.)

YES, I'VE BEEN LOOKING FOR WORK.
(Yeah, some way of working out how to stay on the dole.)

I'M IN BETWEEN JOBS.
(In fact, since I was born.)

I need a counter cheque today because:

I'M STARVING TO DEATH.
(Don't use this while talking with your mouth full or if you're obviously overweight or holding a full shopping bag.)

I'M SICK AND NEED THE MONEY.
(Yeah, I'm sick of having no money.)

I'M GOING ON A ROUND-THE-WORLD TRIP TOMORROW
AND I NEED SOME SPENDING MONEY.

I'VE RUN OUT OF DRUGS.
(For my asthma, that is. Bad time to bring up your heroin
addiction.)

I'VE GOT NO ELECTRICITY OR RUNNING WATER.

S PEEDING

Reasons for speeding
SORRY, OFFICER, I THOUGHT I WAS BEING CHASED BY THE POLICE.

SORRY I'M SPEEDING, OFFICER, BUT I WAS JUST INVOLVED IN A REALLY BAD HIT AND RUN, I'M REALLY PISSED, THE CAR'S UNREGISTERED AND UNROADWORTHY AND I DON'T HAVE A LICENCE, SO I THOUGHT THE QUICKER I'M OFF THE ROAD THE BETTER.

I WAS ON MY WAY TO HOSPITAL.
(Because if I keep driving like this it's only a matter of time before I have an accident.)

MY ACCELERATOR GOT STUCK.
(But luckily it unjammed when I saw three police cars

trying to pull me over.)

MY BRAKES FAILED! LUCKILY I SMASHED INTO YOUR CAR, OFFICER, OR I MIGHT HAVE NEVER STOPPED AT ALL.
(By the way, how long do you think it will be before the 'jaws of life' cut the other officer out of your car?)

Speeding through a tunnel
SORRY, OFFICER, I'M CLAUSTROPHOBIC AND THE TUNNEL WAS FREAKING ME OUT.

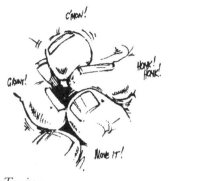

Toe jam

TAXMAN

I ONLY MADE £200 LAST YEAR.
(We believe you, Mr Bond.)

DID I SAY 200? SORRY, I MEANT 2,000,000.

YES, I HAVE 14 CHILDREN TO SUPPORT.
(Just go down to your local school, round up a dozen or two and take them with you.)

TEACHER

I WASN'T TALKING. I WAS MIMING THE ANSWER AND DIDN'T WANT TO UPSTAGE THE REST OF THE CLASS AS I KNOW THEY'RE NOT AS ADVANCED AS MYSELF.

I COULDN'T DO MY HOMEWORK BECAUSE I DIDN'T MAKE IT HOME YESTERDAY. I GOT LOST.

I COULDN'T DO MY HOMEWORK BECAUSE I WAS HELPING UNDERPRIVILEGED HANDICAPPED CHILDREN ALL AFTERNOON AND NIGHT.
(Spit all over your shirt and say that's where they were dribbling on you.)

I DID MY HOMEWORK, BUT THE DOG CHEWED IT UP ON THE WAY TO SCHOOL.
(Shove a piece of paper in your mouth and chew it into a

sopping, gluggy ball. It's a good idea to try and give it to the teacher and watch them freak out.)

I DIDN'T DO MY HOMEWORK BECAUSE I'M HAVING PERSONAL PROBLEMS.
(Yeah, I personally hate doing it.)

I DIDN'T DO MY HOMEWORK BECAUSE MY TUTOR NEVER ARRIVED.
(Yeah, because I don't have one.)

I TRIED FOR HOURS TO DO MY HOMEWORK BUT IT WAS JUST TOO DIFFICULT.
(Works well if you can start crying. Then you can excuse yourself from the classroom and get a free period. This will also give you an excuse for the next day's homework because you won't know what to do.)

I DIDN'T DO MY HOMEWORK BECAUSE I'M HOMELESS.

YOU WANT TO SEE MY HOMEWORK, MY PARENTS WANT TO SEE MY SCHOOL. I'M SO CONFUSED.

NO, I'M NOT CHEWING GUM. I'M GRINDING MY TEETH.

NO, WE WEREN'T FIGHTING. WE WERE JUST GETTING THE DUST OFF EACH OTHER'S FACES WITH OUR KNUCKLES.

THAT'S NOT BLOOD. IT'S THE TOMATO SAUCE FROM MY HOT-DOG.

(This helps if you've actually got a hot-dog. Doesn't work at all if you have a knife in your hand or in your back.)

I'M FEELING SICK. I THINK I MIGHT HAVE TO GO HOME.
(Place the contents of a can of Heinz vegetable soup on the floor and pretend to throw up. It's a good idea before-hand to place a pair of old socks under your armpits. If the spew isn't enough, the smell will get them. This can get you up to a week off school.)

Eat a can of baked beans before class. Fart as loudly as you can in class and then say, 'Oh, no, I've just shit myself' – walk off with a wobbly bum effect. Use this all day in every period.

Leave a message on the teacher's desk saying that there's a bomb in the school – good for one whole day. (PS: Don't sign the note.)

Meeting in later life
WITHOUT YOUR TEACHING SKILLS I WOULDN'T BE WHERE I AM TODAY.
(Terminally unemployed and illiterate.)

TERRORISM

I'M TOO YOUNG TO DIE.
(If the gunman doubts you, start acting childish.)

I'M TOO OLD TO LIVE.
(Act as if death would be an enjoyable experience. Place the gun against your temple. This will take the fun out of it and they will move on to someone else.)

I'M TOO OLD TO DIE.
(If a terrorist asks what you mean by this, shrug and smile sheepishly.)

WE DIDN'T THINK IT WOULD KILL INNOCENT PEOPLE.
(By placing a bomb in a shopping centre.)

TOOTH FAIRY

THE TOOTH FAIRY COULDN'T MAKE IT TONIGHT AS SHE HAD A DENTAL APPOINTMENT.

Tooth pick

U SED C ARS

Buying a car
THIS THING'S A HEAP OF JUNK.
(Don't point to your mother-in-law.)

I THINK IT'S WORTH ABOUT HALF OF THAT.
(Make sure they don't cut it in half.)

I DON'T REALLY LIKE THE CAR.
(Try not to dribble and jump for joy while saying this.)

THE BEST THING ABOUT THAT CAR IS THE AIR IN THE TYRES.

The salesman
IT'S ONLY DONE 3,000 MILES.
(Make sure it's not a brand new car.)

A LITTLE OLD LADY OWNED IT FOR THE PAST 20 YEARS.
SHE ONLY USED IT TO DRIVE TO CHURCH ON SUNDAYS.

SOMEONE ELSE IS REALLY INTERESTED IN IT.
(Yeah, the wreckers.)

THEY SAID THEY WILL BE BACK WITH THE MONEY ANY
MOMENT NOW.
(That was in 1908.)

IT'S GOT NO RUST.
(Or panels or paint.)

PURRS LIKE A KITTEN.
(Runs like a dog.)

THAT HOLE'S SUPPOSED TO BE THERE.
(Make sure it's not where the engine should be.)

I CAN'T HEAR A KNOCKING NOISE.

THAT SMOKE COMING OUT OF THE EXHAUST MEANS IT'S A
HIGH-PERFORMANCE VEHICLE.
(Mmmm . . . yeah, you've got a high chance of being
pulled over for air pollution.)

I'LL BE SORRY TO SEE THIS LITTLE BABY GO.
(Yeah, if it can go.)

THEY DON'T MAKE THEM LIKE THIS ANY MORE.
(Yeah, they burnt the blueprints years ago.)

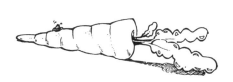

Vegemite

V A L E N T I N E ' S D A Y

Send yourself a least a dozen cards to your work and home with explicit sexual dialogue. Do not do this if you're married or unbelievably ugly.

I'M SORRY I DIDN'T BUY YOU FLOWERS BUT THEY WERE ALL OUT OF LONG-STEMMED ROSES. OTHER FLOWERS WOULDN'T DO JUSTICE TO YOUR EXCEPTIONAL BEAUTY.

DIDN'T YOU RECEIVE YOUR BOUQUET OF FLOWERS TODAY? THAT ROTTEN FLORIST. CAN YOU BELIEVE IT? THAT'S THREE YEARS IN A ROW THEY'VE STUFFED UP.

I PURPOSELY DIDN'T SEND YOU A CARD THIS TIME AS I'M AGAINST WOODCHIPPING.
(Don't tell them this in front of an open fire, or reading the daily paper, or in a log cabin.)

YOUR CARD MUST HAVE GOT LOST IN THE POST.
(Yeah, I lost it before I could post it.)

V

VANDALISING

HOW THE HELL DID THAT CAN OF SPRAY PAINT GET IN MY HAND?

I THOUGHT THEY WANTED PAINTINGS ON THE SIDES OF THEIR TRAINS AND ON THE INSIDES AND THE SEATS.
(Talk in a French accent.)

IT WAS UNBELIEVABLE, OFFICER. THE BRICK JUST SLIPPED OUT OF MY HAND, WENT STRAIGHT THROUGH THE JEWELLER'S WINDOW AND ALL THE RINGS AND WATCHES FELL OUT. I WAS TRYING TO PUT THEM BACK IN. THAT'S HOW I CUT MY HANDS.
(Use this as a last resort.)

OH, I THOUGHT THAT WAS *MY* CAR I WAS SCRAPING THE 20-PENCE PIECE DOWN THE SIDE OF.

(Not your police car.)

I DIDN'T BURN DOWN THE SCHOOL.
(Be sure not to be toasting marshmallows, laughing.)

SIR, I SAW THE PERSON WHO STARTED THE FIRE. THEY RAN OVER THERE.
(Note: If they ask for a description, don't describe yourself. Describe the police officer hassling you and then make a citizen's arrest.)

Cockroach bombs

W A R

These lies are to be used by the leader of the country when wishing to invade a neighbour:

WE NEED MORE LIVING SPACE.

THEY WON'T GIVE US OUR BALL BACK!

THEY STARTED IT.

OURS IS THE ONLY REAL GOD.

WORK EXCUSES

When you're late for work

SORRY I'M LATE – MY ENTIRE FAMILY WAS JUST
INCINERATED IN A HOUSE FIRE!
(Wait for at least six months before trying this one again.
If people are suspicious, hold a mock funeral, take photos
and stick them on the office noticeboard. Send yourself
sympathy cards. If no one still believes you buy an urn.
Put a label on the side reading 'Family Members', then
empty all ashtrays you can find into it. Be sure to remove
the cigarette butts.)

THE TRAFFIC WAS BUMPER TO BUMPER.
(Not too effective if you catch the train.)

THERE WAS A DERAILMENT.
(Make sure you don't drive to work.)

MY PENIS GOT CAUGHT IN MY FLY AND IT TOOK ME THREE-QUARTERS OF AN HOUR TO DELICATELY CUT MY TROUSERS OFF MYSELF, THEN ANOTHER HALF-HOUR ROLLING AROUND THE BED SCREAMING, THEN ANOTHER 40 MINUTES TO GET THE COURAGE TO PUT ANOTHER PAIR OF TROUSERS ON AND DO UP THE FLY.
(Only works for guys, or girls who have injected steroids into their clitoris.)

SORRY, I SLEPT IN.
(Your wife's bed when you left for work.)

SORRY, MY GRANDMOTHER DIED THIS MORNING.
(Note: This only works twice. Ditto with grandfather.)

I SHIT MYSELF ON THE WAY TO WORK.
(Because I was running so late.)

When you won't be in, get someone to ring in for you
RASH WON'T BE IN TODAY – I THINK HE'S DEAD.

RASH WON'T BE IN TODAY – HE'S GOT DIARRHOEA.
(Verbal.)

RASH IS THAT SICK HE CAN'T GET TO THE PHONE.
(Don't ring on a mobile.)

Flipper without his make-up on

X M A S

If you forget to buy the kids a present:

SANTA CLAUS MUST HAVE GOT LOST LAST NIGHT!
(A smart kid will reply: 'Lost? No he wasn't. He spent the entire day at the pub, blew his wages at the bookie's, and then came here and spent the entire evening screwing mum.')

Plead ignorance
XMAS . . . YOU MUST BE KIDDING?
(As a final ploy, immediately convert to Islam and insist that Xmas is Western propaganda. Hijack a plane to further convince them.)

IT'S SO GREAT TO SEE ALL MY RELATIVES AGAIN.

X-RATED SEX SHOPS

I'LL HAVE A PACKET OF EXTRA LARGE CONDOMS, PLEASE.
(You wish.)

COULD YOU CHANGE A £50 NOTE INTO £1 COINS? IT'S
FOR THE CIGARETTE MACHINE.
(There's no need to lie – the bloke knows you're going
straight into the gripper's booth.)

GIVE ME ONE OF THOSE BLOW-UP DOLLS, PLEASE. IT'S FOR
MY MATE.
(Sure.)

Fly spray

Yourself

Lying to yourself
You can tell yourself you don't lie to yourself and there's the proof – you just did. I'm sure we've all said these a few times.

Dieting
I'M GOING ON A DIET.
(First thing in the morning.)

Next day
I'LL DEFINITELY START NEXT MONDAY.

Next Monday
STUFF IT – I'M NOT THAT FAT ANYWAY.

I'M NOT THAT FAT ANYWAY.

(Who are you kidding? You're a pig.)

Smoking
I'M GIVING UP SMOKING.
(Starting tomorrow.)

Next day
OH, ONE WON'T HURT.

That night
I'VE GOT TO HAVE ONE WHILE I'M HAVING A DRINK.

Two hours later
FUCK IT. WHO CARES?

Four hours later
YOU'RE ROLLING JOINTS.

Drinking
Next day
MASSIVE HANGOVER – I'M NEVER DOING THAT AGAIN.

That night
WHOSE SHOUT?
(And do you know where I can buy some pot/and has anyone got a ciggy?)

Exercise
I'M STARTING BACK UP AT THE GYM ON MONDAY.

First Monday
OH, I'M TOO BUSY THIS WEEK, NEXT WEEK FOR SURE.
(Probably on the dole.)

Second Monday
OH, THIS IS GREAT. I'M JOINING UP FOR A YEAR. I'LL COME
EVERY DAY.

Tuesday
OH, I'M TOO SORE TO GO TODAY.

Wednesday
I'LL BE BACK.

Thursday
I'M NOT GOING ANY MORE – I DON'T WANT TO BE
MUSCULAR AND BULKY.

Age 10
I'VE GOT TO DO THAT ONE DAY.

Age 40
I'VE GOT TO DO THAT ONE DAY.

Age 80
I'VE GOT TO DO THAT ONE DAY.

Age 90
Why didn't you do it?
OH, I DIDN'T HAVE TIME.

Gambling

I HAVEN'T GOT A GAMBLING ADDICTION. CAN YOU LEND ME £20, THOUGH? OH, COME ON, I'LL BET YOU £50 I GIVE IT BACK TO YOU.

I HAVEN'T GOT A GAMBLING ADDICTION, NOW SHUT UP, I CAN'T HEAR THE RACE.

WORD

A four-letter word

ZOMBIE

If meeting one
YOU LOOK STRANGELY ATTRACTIVE IN THE MOONLIGHT.

IT'S SUCH A PLEASURE.
(While thinking this is the last blind date I go on.)

If the situation looks dangerous, strike up a casual conversation with the zombie. Ask if being buried alive limits their social life. Mention the career possibilities in the public service. Ask which cemetery they live in. Promise to drop in sometime. If all else fails, tell a joke. 'Two zombies walked into a bar', etc.

The End!